CW00369752

THE AWFULLY GOOD CAT JOKE BOOK

Jokes by David Jacobs
Illustrated by Trevor Dunton

metro

First published in Great Britain in 1996 by Metro Books
(an imprint of Metro Publishing Limited),
19 Gerrard Street, London W1V 7LA

Trevor Dunton is hereby identified as the illustrator of
this work in accordance with Section 77 of the
Copyright, Designs and Patents Act 1988

David Jacobs is hereby identified as the author of this
work in accordance with Section 77 of the Copyright,
Designs and Patents Act 1988

British Library Cataloguing in Publication Data. A CIP
record of this book is available on request from the
British Library.

ISBN 1 900512 10 6

Design by Richard Burgess

Printed and bound in Italy by L.E.G.O. Vicenza

Q: What's a cat's favourite catch-phrase?
A: HAVE A MICE DAY

Q: What is a cat's favourite colour?
A: PURRPLE

Q: What do cats use for cutting the grass?
A: A LAWN MEWER

Q: How do cats enter heaven?
A: **THROUGH THE PURRLY GATES**

Q: What do Jewish cats celebrate?
A: PUSSOVER

Q: What happens to cats that don't shave?
A: **WHISKERS**

Q: What do cats who smoke
   heavily suffer from?
A: CATAAR

cough!

Q: What describes a cat in a panic?
A: A CAT FLAP

Q: What do cats read over breakfast?
A: A TABBYLOID MEWSPAPER

Q: Why do cats never go hungry in Reykjavik?
A: BECAUSE ITS IN MICELAND

REYKJAVIK BAR & GRILL
MENU
EGG FRIED MICE
MICE CREAM
+ PLAIN MICE
CHIPS

Q: How do cats travel on the water?
A: BY CATAMARAN

Q: What do cats eat to keep
   themselves regular?
A: MEWSLI AND PURRUNES

Q: Who is the most evil cat in history?
A: CATILLA THE HUN

Q: What is a cat's favourite sauce?
A: TOMATO CATCHUP

Q: What line of Shakespeare best describes
a cat's favourite activity?
A: 'TO SLEEP, PURRCHANCE TO DREAM' *(Hamlet*

Q: How do you describe a cat
   doing nothing in particular?
A: PUSSY-FOOTING AROUND

Q: What do you call a sexually deviant cat?
A: A PURRVERT

Q: What are a cat's favourite vegetables?
A: PURRSNIPS AND SPINACH PURREE

Q: What is a cat's favourite firework?
A: A CATHERINE WHEEL

Q: What is a cat's favourite
   form of creative writing?
A: PURRETRY

I wish
My dish
was full
of fish....

Q: What do you call a cat with
   managerial responsibilities?
A: AN EXECATIVE

DR JEKYLL'S CAT

BEFORE

Q: What does a cat use for experiments
   in the chemistry lab?
A: A BUNSEN PURRNER

AFTER

Q: What is a cat's favourite drink?
A: A GOOD VINTAGE PURRGUNDY

Q: What is the capital of Catland?
A: CATMANDU

Q: What do cats in love say to each other?
A: THE FEELINE'S MEWTUAL

* How about a fish supper then back to my place?

** I'd rather be savaged by a rabid Rottweiler

Q: What is a cat's favourite
   theatrical performance?
A: *THE MOUSETRAP*

Q: What do you call a female cat who
   succumbs easily to male advances?
A: A PUSS OVER

Q: Where do cats go for their holidays?
A: MOGGYDISHU

Q: How do cats sing?
A: STACATTO

Q: Why are cats no good on computers?
A: BECAUSE THEY ALWAYS
   SWALLOW THE MOUSE